Lonely

I'm just a lonely artist
On this mortal path
Got to make myself a living
With the life I have
Taken from me more than what I got
Travelled rough along the way
Slept underneath the stars
I gave up the drinking
Dancing with pennies at my feet
Writing poems on my phone
Painting on the kitchen floor
I paint for money
I will paint for free
I never thought I could see this world
Pack up bags each summer
Make some art along the way
Carrying the weight of judgement
They want me to be more than what they are
To be much more than what I am
And I've given everything I've got
But everything they think I am
I am not

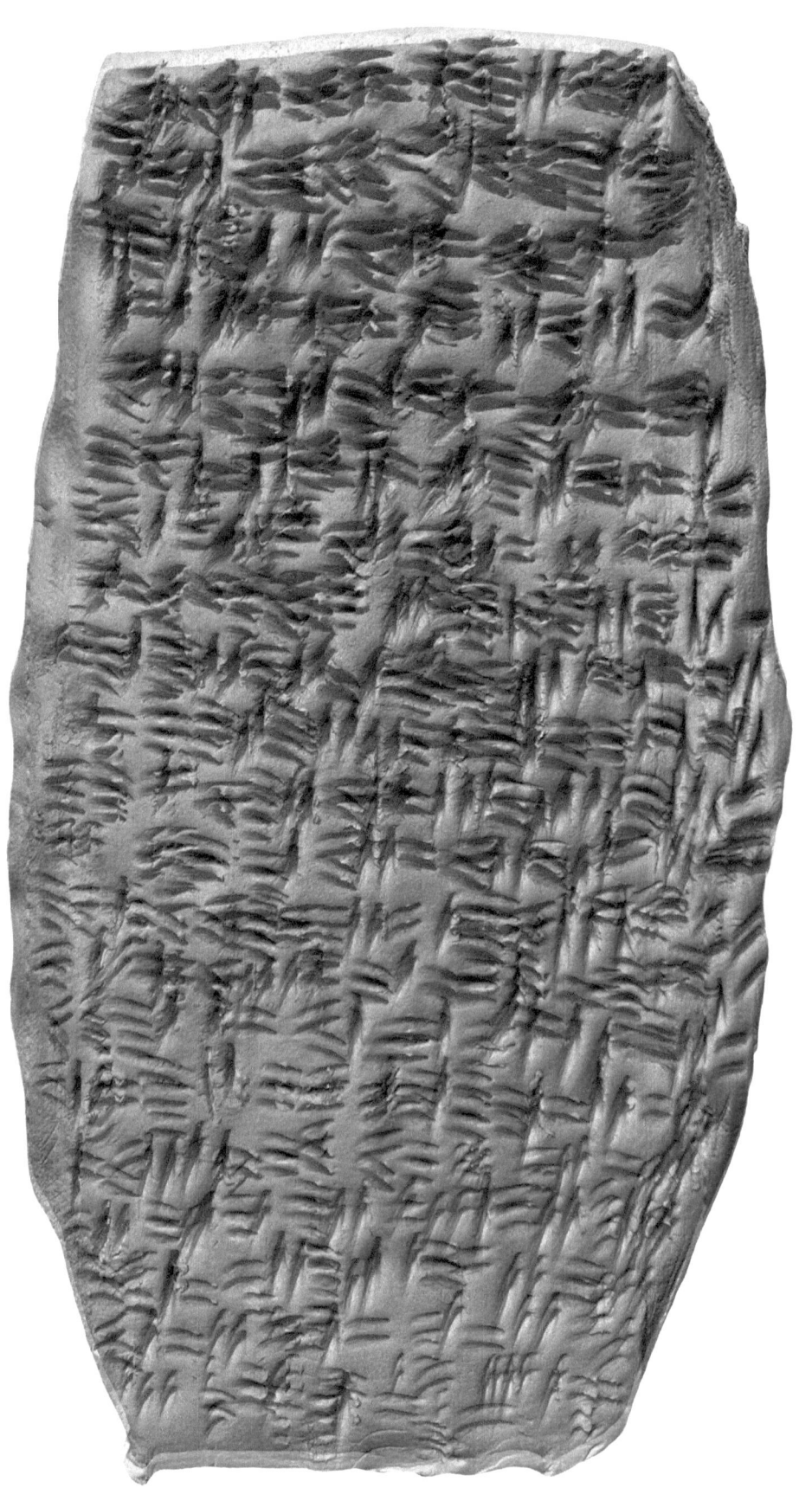

The fool

Not been here long
Done all the stupid stuff
That people do
I have sunk
Learnt to swim
Pulled under by the current
And walked on water
Felt the sun
Danced in the rain
I play the part
Of the fool
I dance on the rainbow
Never searching for gold

Yellow Paint

You are the alcohol through my veins.
The rips in my heart
The key to the secret passages in my mind.
My map to nowhere when I feel lost.
You are the green in my eyes
the taste in my mouth
the blood in my womb.
the fingerprint stains on my breasts
You are my Yellow Paint.

♡ van Gogh

Love Spell

I wish upon you burning love
Agony of violet love
And insane desire
You will suffer
How I suffer
Horrific love sickness
Curse your eyes green
Like mine are for you
Erotic magical spell
Bring you to me
Our hearts pinned together
Our bodies bound to another
For all immortality

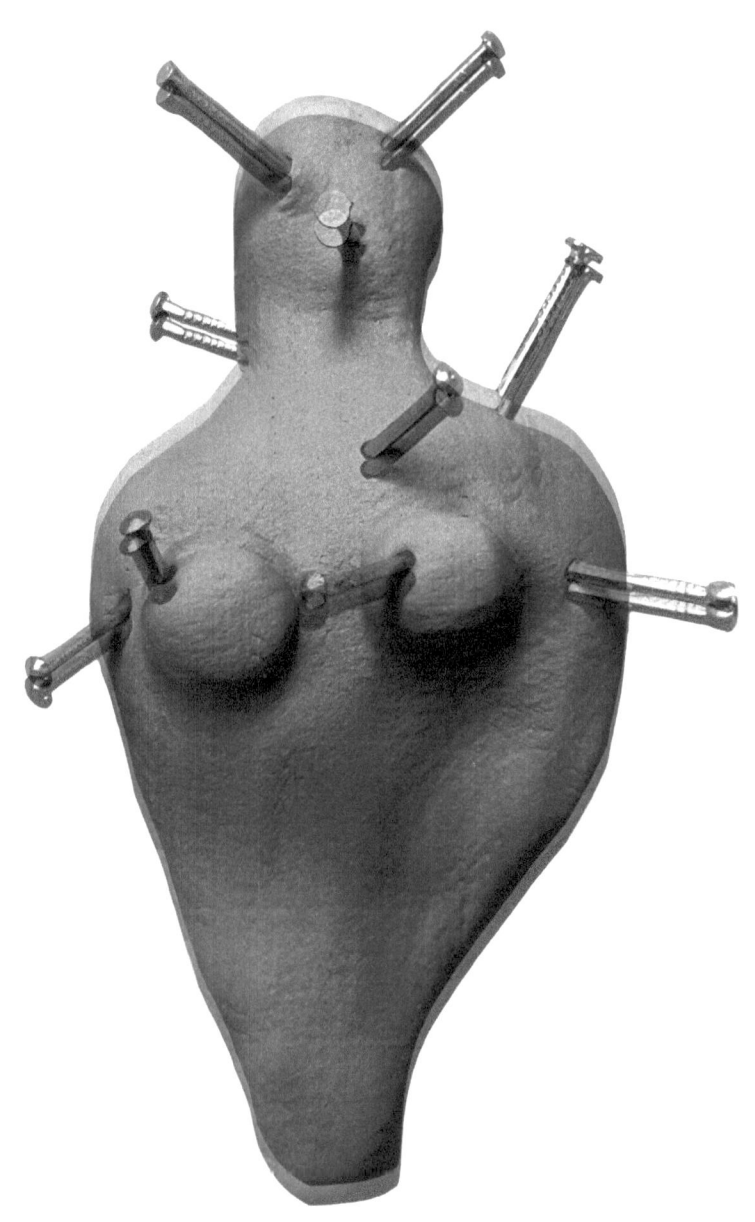

Valhalla

I draw the curtains again
And I worry I can't save myself
Each month gets harder
The wolf woman awakes
The wild inside I can't repress
I try to hide
I've tried the cures
For being a woman
To fit in with the world
Swallowing pills
Numb my pleasure
Numb my pain
Yet it's not enough
My skin crawls in agony
My heart stabs
Mouth speaks cruelly
What is this inside of me ?
Battling ghosts in my mind
Pass over my skin
Made friends with the past
Covered up the bruises
Created new delusions
Voices inside my skull laugh
I see when I close my eyes
Butterflies torture my stomach
My breath stolen away
Fighting with myself
Fighting with flowers
I pull my hair to the floor
Watch skin turn red
Watch water turn to blood
Self loathing and loving
Don't let her win
Don't let her win
I'm so exhausted
I'm tired of being so exhausted
Wolf woman is stronger than me
When my time is up
Please remember me as a warrior

Medusas Redemption

Stole away her innocence
No longer a priestess
She hid away her beauty
Cut her long glossy hair
To reduce temptation
She covered her body
So eyes won't scar her skin
She closed her mouth
To drink no more
Shut herself off from trust
And self exiled
Her misery grew stronger
She lived with pain
Thoughts grew thicker roots
She lived with anger
Her body weaker
She lived with Jealousy
Her pain poured out on to others
Her piousness delusions and tongue
Turned who she loved to stone
She didn't know how to not live alone
Petrified love to rubble
She begged please
Take my head
I don't want my head
I can't stand this head
Soaked in another's sins
Turned inner violence
Please take these thoughts
She begs on knees
Please take my head

And he took her hand

I'm a fucking mess

You always stick around
You witnessed everything
The sides of me no one else ever sees
I put us through shit
You wear my sins
You hold my pain
I want to make you proud
But I've let you down

She fell in love with a man that was nothing like her father. He was the enemy of him. Her father gave her away like property. He wanted nothing to do with the cost of her existence. She was a failure, a lost cause and a artist. She was a stubborn bitch that drank whiskey. How dare she choose a poor man over her Father. She choose a hand to hold instead of money. She choose love over pain. The man she dreamt of with a free spirit and long flowing hair was here. He existed. He didn't follow the rules and behaved in ways she never knew you could. She didn't understand this man. He was like no-one she had every met before. He was soft, forgiving and supportive.

After every fight she realised he was always right. She learnt it the hard way. He was smart. Smart in a different way. He knew a lot more about life than her. He was intelligent and creative. Someone who didn't draw within the lines. Who didn't bend to accommodate a life he didn't want. Who was more stubborn than her. Who knew her more than herself. Who looked after her better than herself. Who saw her worth more than herself. He held the door open to the places that seemed out of reach. He held her when she cried and he let her make stupid mistakes. He supported her through everything she wanted to do. No matter his opinion on it. He let her make the bad choices. The good choices. He let her find her own way and blossom in to the black throned rose that she was destined to be.

[All iCloud]   Done

Your love Directs like the North Star in the Night
It is salvation and torment
Stronger than a gilded cage
Worth more than any treasure
It burns brighter than the midday sun
And I love you more

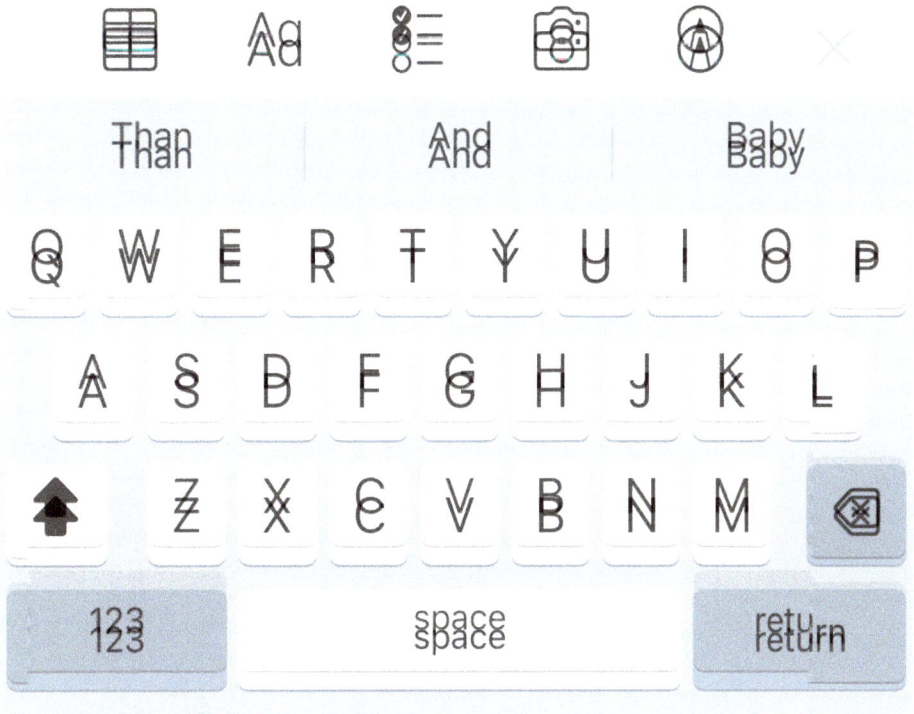

Penny for my thoughts

Tell my secrets
Tell my story
Stabbed in the back
Don't give in
Be honest
Be pure
Be soft
Exposed heart to stone
Self sabotage
Self rescue
Let out emotions
Mouth faster than thought
Sober mind
Drink cant soak it up
Let it out
Fix whats broken
Learning in time
Only mend in gold

Knight in dirty docs

Come to me, my knight
Hold my hand
Turn down the light

Stroke my hair
Run your fingers across my lips
Pretend that you care

🖤 for my man

You bring 🥀
🏃‍♀️ fingers on 👄
Bruises on 🍑
From ❤️ made
👅 me
🩸 for you
☠️ for you
💔 without

Virtual Dolls

Cut pieces of me off
Put chunks back on
Tell me I'm imperfect
Tell me I'm wrong

Cure my wounds
By digging more
What makes me beautiful
Makes me sore

Change my colours
To be seen
No longer me
My own unique Queen

Missing part

I know what it feels like
To loose
I wont let that happen
You do nothing wrong
Forgiveness my weakness
You're irreplaceable
I'm insane without you
Death to be apart
Together like heaven and hell
Waiting to dance in the afterlife
Lay on your chest
Heartbeat comforter
More than meets the eye
A rare gem
You place metal on fingers
But you are
My greatest treasure

< All iCloud

Love you more than words can express. Love your wild untamed mind. Love the sparkle in the tempest of your eyes. Love your power and your strength. Love how you paint your colours upon beige reality. I love you until the end of days and further still. I love you completely and always will.

Once upon a time

Makeup running down my face
Dinner going cold
Showing your mistakes
You lie to save me
It only hurts more
Can't press rewind
But now we walk away
I live with pain
Filled my glass up
Its overflowed
A stubborn daydreamer
But so are you
Jealously
You don't want to know
Doesn't matter who's wrong or right
We both loose
You see someone in me
Loved up vagabonds
We don't give up
Giving up is not our way

Stone Cold Bitch

Got to be tough
And be stronger
Pain to stories
Ears burn
Jester privileges
At a cost
Stabs in the back
While holding hands
Blood runs cold
Beating heart turns stone

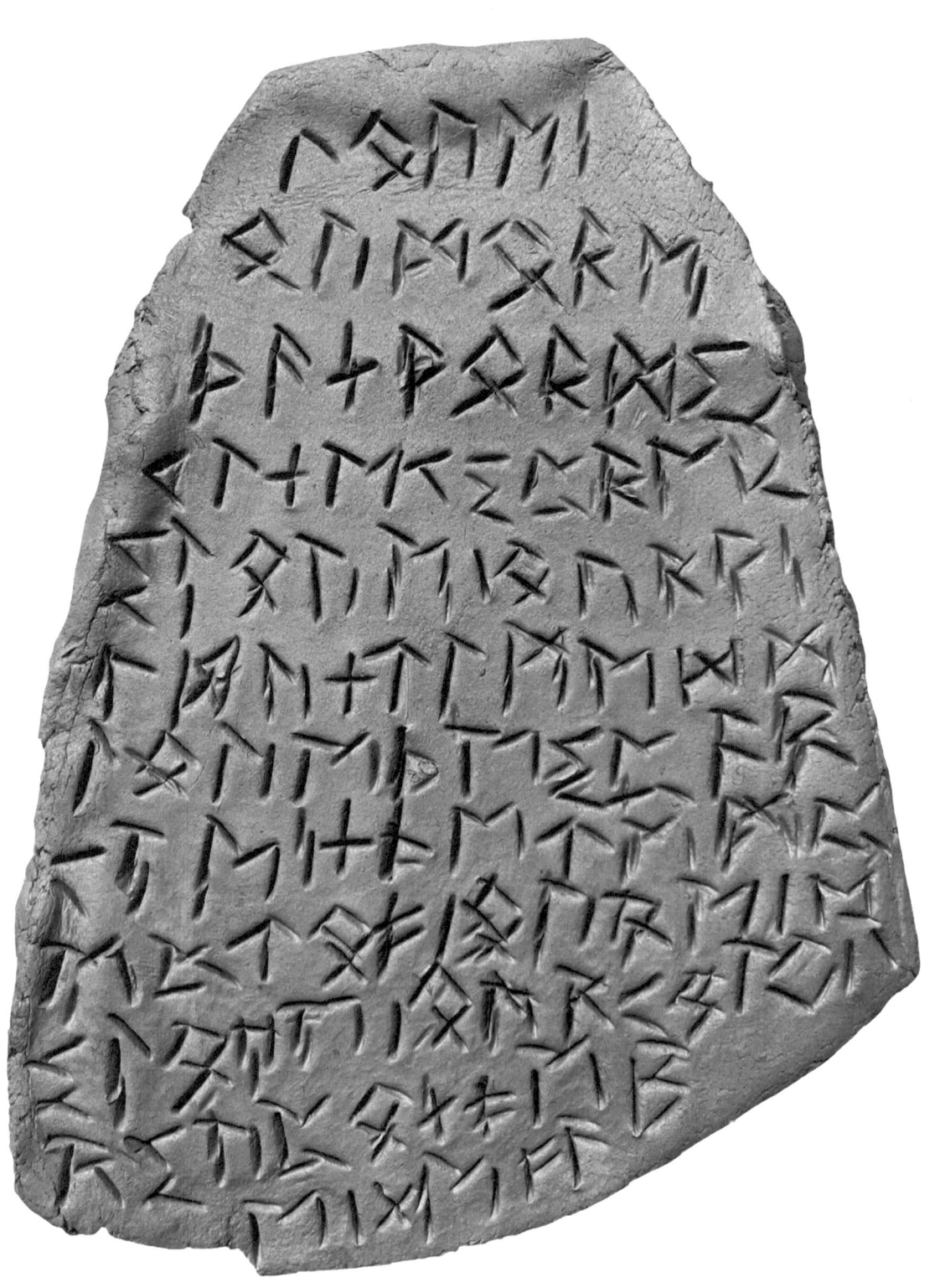

Take the side of love
Your untamed side
Fierce as a wolf
That overcomes me like the night

Put it down

I didn't know it existed
But now I need it
I need it like air
It's motivation
It's education
A friend
A life line
Enemy
Life tastes different
Knowing more exists
It bite's
My innocence gone
Instead of hands
I hold a thing
Scroll through lives
Ache for what I don't need
Commodity of Envy
Virtual world cherrypicking
Scrapbook into the mind
Filter tinted perception
To do more
Or be more
Look smaller
Look bigger
Never do and be all
Mortality unfulfilled
All the stories
Stalking a life I won't have

Cursed

I was cursed in pain
Named a Witch
Lived like a gypsy
Field abode
I was different
I wasn't enough
Gained their eyes
Instead of my own
My freedom
Stolen by thieves
Acting like them
In a self made cage
This is not living
A life of envy
A life of sameness
it's a crime

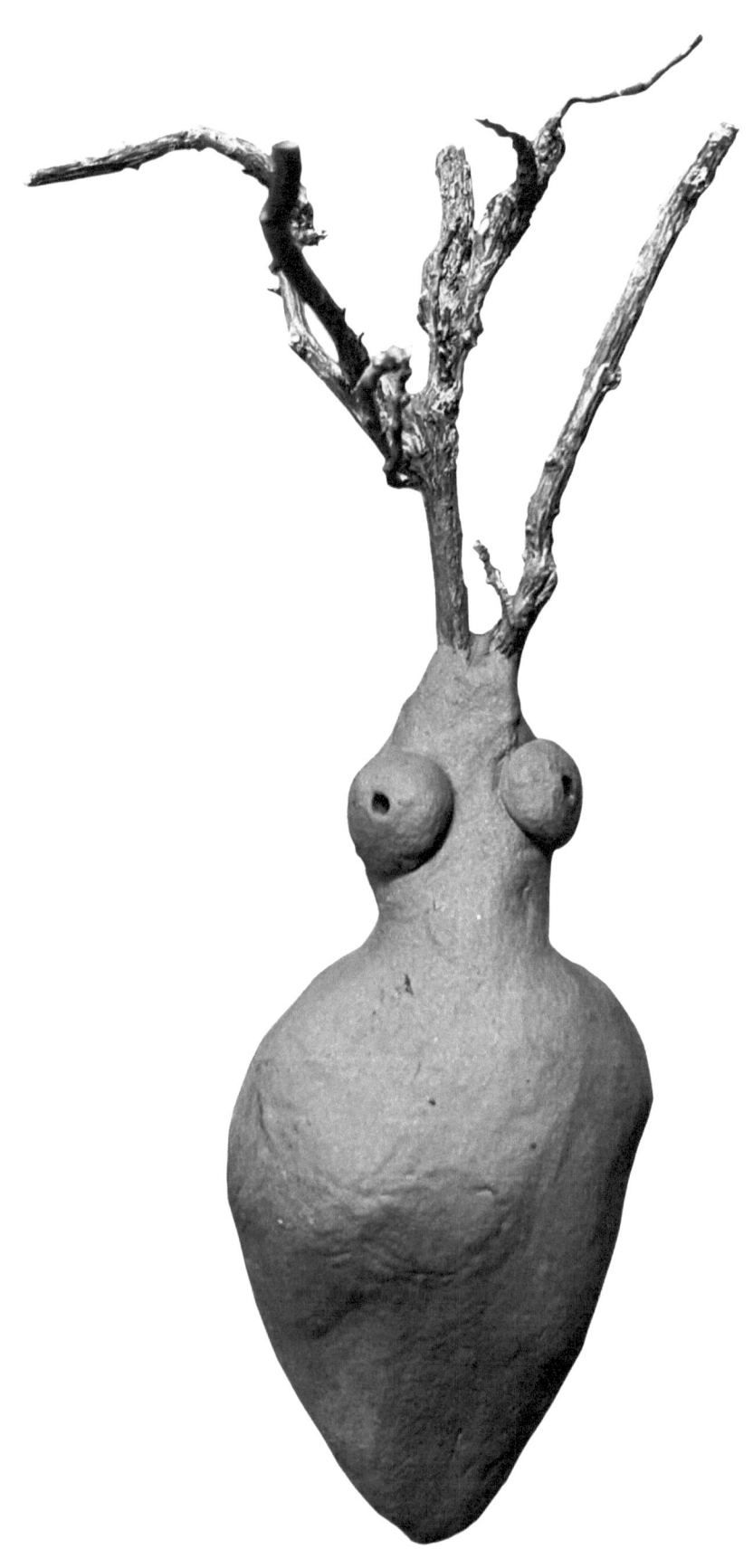

Became mother

It hurts to love
Strong emotions
Weak hands
Tear in eyes
Stabbing heart
Life is painful
Mortality is thin
You're not alone
I'm not alone
Keeping you safe
My venture
Once protected in womb
Pressure of life
A privilege to have
Just a soul passenger travelling through
Now belonging to the world
I will hold your hand throughout life
When my voice is a whinge
My opinion not wanted
You can't stand me
I'll stand nearby
I will love you

www.ingramcontent.com/pod-product-compliance
Lightning Source LLC
Chambersburg PA
CBHW051953210526
45473CB00024B/2381